# Quest for Awesomeness

## From Ordinary to Extraordinary

# Quest for Awesomeness

*From Ordinary to Extraordinary*

**Marsha Ferrick Heiden, PhD., BCC**

*Author*

**Maria Berg**

*Artist*

# Quest for Awesomeness

From Ordinary to Extraordinary

Written by *Marsha Ferrick Heiden, PhD., BCC*
Illustrated by *Maria Berg*

*Marsha Ferrick Heiden, PhD, BCC*
*Amara Quest, Inc.*
*8322 State Route 305*
*Garrettsville, OH 44231*

http://www.amaraquest.com

*To:*

Maria, who is as aweome as her work!

Maria Berg is portrait and figurative artist living in Bruchköbel, Germany, near the home of the Brothers Grimm. For as long as she can remember, Maria has lived on stories and fairy tales, which have formed her understanding of herself and her life's journey.

Her goal as an artist it to reflect and to reveal life's beauty through images that touch the heart and inspire the viewer to seek beyond that which is seen. For this purpose, she dedicates herself not only to the act of painting itself, but also to communing with nature and to studying the great works of art created by the artists of the past.

Maria is a graduate of the National University of Arts, Bucharest, Romania, and has accomplished more than 200 portraits, many of which now reside in private collections throughout the world. She can be reached at: www.maria-berg-art.de.

# Contents

# What is a Quest?

A quest is a journey. This quest is a journey to find your awesomeness. This is an inner quest to locate that which is already in you, and to allow you to find, embrace, grow, and utilize your awesomeness in your day to day life. Awesomeness is a key to mastery, and to living your life on your terms. Enjoy the journey!

## Seeker's Name

# The Preparing

Describe three moments in your life that you would attribute to your awesomeness.

1. 

2. 

3. 

What made these moments stand out for you?

What have you incorporated into your life from your past moments of awesomeness?

How could you use more of what you have learned from these awesome moments to assist you in making future changes?

List five adjectives that describe you when you are "AWESOME"

*Physically*

1. 

2. 

3. 

4. 

5.

## Emotionally

1. 
2. 
3. 
4. 
5. 

## Mentally

1. 
2. 
3. 
4. 
5.

What are you learning and accepting about yourself as you write about your awesomeness?

# The Discovery

## Your Focus

- A positive connection with yourself.
- Lead yourself to an empowered perspective.
- Affirm a sense of the possible.
- Cultivate and support a belief in a positive future.

## Your Challenge

1. Describe what you consider awesomeness to be.

2. Write a definition, phrase or quote to describe it.

3. When have you displayed awesomeness? Describe each situation which required you to be awesome.

4. Describe situations which do not require awesomeness?

5. What do you think are the characteristics that distinguish awesome individuals from those not operating out of their awesomeness?

6. What attitudes or beliefs do you consider to be the opposite of each of the above characteristics?

7. What do you consider to be the observable behaviors associated with each of the awesomeness characteristics you listed in #5 above?

8. What do you think co-workers or peers would contend to be characteristics of an awesome individual and the observable behaviors associated with them?

9. Discuss the characteristics and behaviors of awesomeness with one or two of your colleagues or peers. What did you find out?

```


```

10. Write a definition of awesomeness for yourself.

```


```

11. Be aware of when you were awesome today and take note of it.

```


```

# The Dream

## Your Focus

- Encourage yourself to create images of possibilities.
- Give voice to your possibilities.
- Affirm your dreams.

## Your Challenge

1. Imagine one night while you were asleep a miracle occurred. When you wake you are *"awesome"* as you described earlier, in all situations that required awesomeness. How would you know you were awesome?

2. What is different?

3. What has changed in your habits?

4. Who will be the first to notice these changes?

5. What will they say or do, and how will you respond?

6. Make a list of what will remain the same because it already contributes to your awesomeness.

7. What habits will you continue?

8. How will you increase the habits that contribute to your awesomeness?

I will

I will

I will

I will

I will

# The Map

## Focus

- Bring your dream into focus.
- Affirm the reality of your dream.
- Support your mindful choices and actions.

## Your Challenge

1. How will you act differently to make the dream you created work of your awesomeness a reality?

2. How best can you develop your awesomeness?

3. Are there significant others' who you feel will play a crucial role in the development of your awesomeness?

4. What do you think these individuals do to help? What do they not do?

5. Are there any techniques or methods that you have experienced which you feel influences the development of awesomeness?

6. Think of someone you know who you would characterize as being awesome. How do you think they developed their awesomeness?

7. List three key components to increasing your awesomeness.

8. Which component will you start to create or enhance.

# Your Destiny

## Your Focus

- Recognize you are living your dream in the present.
- Expand your capacity to create your dream.
- Support yourself when the going gets tough.

## The Holy Grail

1. Reflect on what you really want and where you are right now regarding your awesomeness, what do you see as the most significant changes you could make that would help you get what you want?

2. What one small change could you make right now, no matter how small that would improve your awesomeness? The change does not have to be physical action it could be a shift in thinking or attitude.

3. Just try it. Do this small change today that will move you in the direction of what you want and when it feels comfortable or becomes a habit, consider making another small change using the same small steps. What will that next small step be?

For Additional Titles:

http://www.amaraquest.com

www.ingramcontent.com/pod-product-compliance
Lightning Source LLC
Chambersburg PA
CBHW041239040426

42445CB00004B/78